MANNERS IN GOD'S HOUSE
First Prayers and First Missal

Neumann Press
Charlotte, North Carolina

MANNERS IN GOD'S HOUSE

CONTENTS

These books, originally published under three separate covers, were first issued in 1950.

ISBN: 978-0-911845-19-8

Printed and bound in the United States of America.

Neumann Press
Charlotte, North Carolina
www.NeumannPress.com
2013

LET'S PRAY

First Prayers for Little Catholics

SELECTED AND EXPLAINED BY
SISTER M. JULIANA, O.P., OF THE MARYKNOLL SISTERS

ILLUSTRATED BY CHARLOT BYJ

IMPRIMATUR:

✠ JOHN G. MURRAY

ARCHBISHOP OF ST. PAUL

DECEMBER 27, 1951

CATECHETICAL GUILD
EDUCATIONAL SOCIETY

ST. PAUL, MINNESOTA

NEUMANN PRESS

THE SIGN OF THE CROSS...

THE GREATEST SIGN OF ALL

WE call it the Sign of the Cross because we make it like a cross. It stands for the cross on which Christ died. This sign shows we are Christians.

In the Name of the Father *and of the Son* *and of the Holy Ghost.* *Amen.*

THIS greatest sign tells us that there is only one God. But it also shows that we believe there are three persons in God. And it tells us the names of these Three Persons — the Father and the Son and the Holy Ghost.

GOD the Father is the Creator. That means He made the earth and everything out of nothing. He made us, too, and He loves us. Jesus is His Son.

GOD the Son is the Second Person we name in the Sign of the Cross. We also call Him Jesus Christ. God the Father sent Him down from heaven to save us from our sins. He was born as a little baby in a stable at Bethlehem.

In the Name of the Father and of the Son

THE Holy Ghost is the Third Person. He comes into our hearts to make us holy. He is love and sweetness and life.

And of the Holy Ghost. Amen.

The Sign of the Cross

reminds us that Jesus died on a cross. When God created the first people, He created them to be good and to be happy with Him. But they did something bad right away and they had to be punished. God the Father wanted them to be happy, so He sent His Son Jesus, Who was willing to take their punishment. Jesus died on the Cross for us — and for everybody. When we make the Sign of the Cross, we thank God for sending His Son to take our punishment and make us holy again.

We make the
Sign of the
Cross before
we pray, eat, sleep, or work. When we
make the Sign of the Cross carefully,
and with love, bad thoughts go away
and we grow
to love God
more. Devils
fear the cross
and run away
from its sign.

THE OUR FATHER

JESUS taught us this prayer. He is the Son of God. He told us that God is our Father, too. So when we pray "Our Father" we are praying together with Jesus and all Christians every-where.

*   *   *   *Our Father*   *   *   *

HEAVEN is God's home. God wants us to be with Him in heaven some day. Nobody cries there because everybody is happy. Jesus has a place for us in heaven. If we love Him, we will go there and be happy, too.

THE Name of God is wonderful and holy. The angels bow down whenever they hear this name. Everyone who prays loves the Holy Name of God. We want everybody in the whole world to know that name and love it.

---

*   *   *Hallowed be Thy name*   *   *

A FAMILY has a father for its head. A country has a president. Everything must have a head in order to work the way it should. People are good and happy only when they have God for their head. We all pray together so that the whole world will accept God as its head. Then we shall have peace and happiness.

*   *   *Thy kingdom come*   *   *

IN heaven, everyone is happy. They are happy because they do what God wants. He wants them to love Him and to love each other. We want everyone on earth to love one another, too. Then the whole world will be happy. It will be more like heaven!

* *Thy will be done on earth as it is in heaven.* *

WE ask God to give us all we need. The world has many homeless and hungry people. We pray for them and also we think of the orphans and helpless old people. We ask God to take care of them all.

Give us this day our daily bread. And forgive us

MANY people are bad. Either they do not know God or they do not love Him. When bad men nailed Jesus to the cross, He said: "Father, forgive them." If we love everyone, then we will forgive them whenever they hurt us. Then we shall be like Jesus.

Our trespasses as we forgive those who trespass against us

HERE on earth there are many troubles. But the worst trouble of all is to be separated from God by sin.

* * *And lead us not into temptation* * *

18

WE ask God to keep us and all men from wars and sadness. We beg Him to take care of all people so that they will all know Him, and love Him, and come to heaven with Him at last.

✳   *But deliver us from evil.*   ✳   ✳

WITH Jesus and the angels and all people who pray, I say "Amen." Amen means "Please, dear God, make all these wishes come true."

＊   ＊   ＊   *Amen.*   ＊   ＊   ＊

THE FIRST PEOPLE

WHEN God made the first people, He called them Adam and Eve. He made a beautiful spot for them to live. God also gave them grace. Grace is something God gives people to make their souls holy and please Him. Adam and Eve were happy because they were holy.

BUT Adam and Eve did not stay holy. They committed a sin and lost the grace God had given them. God made them leave their beautiful home.

SINCE men didn't have grace any more, nobody could go to heaven. The door of heaven was closed. But God loved men so much He promised them that some day they would be able to get grace again. He said He would send His own son, Jesus, to open the door of heaven.

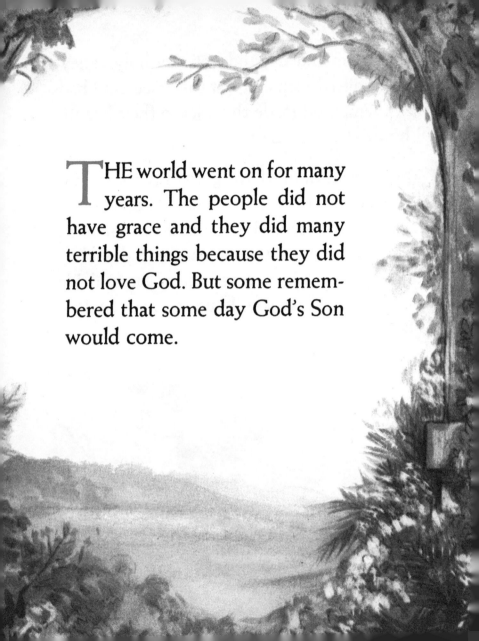

THE world went on for many years. The people did not have grace and they did many terrible things because they did not love God. But some remembered that some day God's Son would come.

THEN, at last, came the time for Jesus to be born. God chose a woman named Mary to be the Mother of Jesus. God created her the best person who ever lived.

THE HAIL MARY

ONE day an angel came to Mary. He was sent by God to tell her that she was to be Jesus' Mother! He told her that she was full of grace. She was the first person since Adam and Eve who had the life of grace in her soul.

Hail Mary, full of grace

MARY knew that Jesus was God and would bring grace back to all the people. So she told the angel that she was willing to become the Mother of Jesus!

*   *   *The Lord is with thee*   *   *

AS the Mother of Jesus, Mary is the queen of heaven and earth. When we pray the Hail Mary, she takes our prayers to Jesus. Since Jesus is her Son, He listens to everything she tells Him.

* *Blessed art thou among women* *

WHEN Jesus was born, Mary was very happy. She knew that this little Baby was the Son of God, and that one day He would open the door of heaven.

And blessed is the fruit of thy womb, Jesus.   ✳

GOD the Father sent God the Son to die for us and open the door of heaven. Mary is the Mother of God the Son whose name is Jesus.

✳ *Holy Mary, Mother of God, pray for us sinners,*

MARY knew that Jesus died for the sin of Adam and Eve and for the sins of every person who would ever live. We need Jesus' help and Mary's prayers so we will be happy forever in heaven.

Now and at the hour of our death. Amen. ✳

PRAYER BEFORE MEALS

Bless us, O Lord,
and these Thy gifts,
which we are about to receive
from Thy bounty,
through Christ our Lord. Amen.

PRAYER AFTER MEALS

We give Thee thanks for all Thy benefits,
O Almighty God,
Who livest and reignest forever.
May the souls of the faithful departed,
through the mercy of God,
rest in peace. Amen.

PRAISING GOD

Glory be to the Father
and to the Son,
and to the Holy Ghost.
As it was in the beginning,
is now
and ever shall be,
world without end.
Amen.

GOOD MANNERS
IN GOD'S HOUSE

BY SISTER MARY ST. PAUL OF MARYKNOLL
PICTURES BY BRINTON TURKLE

Nihil obstat: WALTER H. PETERS, *Censor*

Imprimatur: ✠ WILLIAM O. BRADY, *Archbishop of St. Paul*

January 1, 1959

A First Book for Little Catholics

In the park, you play games.
You shout and run and jump.
This is the right way to act
when you play.

You act in other ways at home.
You act in other ways at school.

Still, it is fun to be noisy.
It is fun to play.
It makes you feel good.
But you can feel good, too,
when you are very, very
QUIET.

Can you think of a place
that is very quiet?
It is a place that everyone loves.
This special place is God's house.
It is the church.

Every church is the palace of your King.
Your King is Jesus.
And Jesus is God.
　Sometimes you visit Jesus, your King,
in His palace.
Then you act in special ways.

You remember that you are going
to the palace of a great King.
That is why you want to have
a clean body,
clean clothes,
and tidy hair.
You want to be your very best
when you visit Jesus.
He is your God and your King.

Jesus loves you very much.
The door of His palace is always open.
You go in softly and quietly.
Near the door you find holy water.
You put your fingertip in it.

You do not waste the holy water.
You make a big Sign of the Cross with it.
And you say:

"In the name of the Father, and of the Son,
and of the Holy Ghost. Amen."

Now you are in the palace
of the great King, our Lord Jesus Christ.
He is there on the altar.
He sees you walk softly down the aisle.
And He watches you with love.

You are no longer just a plain child.
You are a special child of God, your King.
Every boy is a prince.
Every girl is a princess in the Church of God.

On you go till you come to the place
where you will sit.
You bend your right knee before Jesus.
You make sure your knee touches the floor.
Then you walk all the way into the seat.

This pleases your King
because He wants you to leave room for others.

You love God very much.
You want many other people to come to Him.
So you leave space for them.
Then they will not have to crawl over you.

Sometimes everyone seems quiet in church,
but everyone is talking to Jesus.
They are talking a special kind of talk.
And Jesus can hear everyone at once.
That is because He is God.

You can send messages to God
just by thinking.
The message He likes most is:
"My God, I love You."

Prayer books help you to learn
how to talk to God.
A rosary, a crucifix, holy pictures,
and statues help you to think of God.

At Mass, the priest dresses in long robes.
They are like the robes that Jesus wore.
You watch the priest,
and this helps you to think of Jesus.

Your prayer book about the Mass
will tell you what to do.
You stand when Father enters
and again when he leaves.
And you stand up straight.

When the altar boy rings the bell,
you kneel up straight.
Some boys and girls do this very well.
Keep practicing.
You will learn to do it well, too.

Babies cannot sit still very long.
They are always looking this way and that.
But you are not a baby.
You will not look this way and that in church.
You will look straight ahead
and keep your eyes on your King.

Practice the right way of acting
in God's house.
Teach others to act in the right way.
Then God will know you are His friend.
He will watch you leave the church.
And He will let you take His happiness
with you.
He will help you to be happier than ever.

RULES FOR VISITORS TO THE KING

1. Boys take off their hats in church.
They tip their hats when they pass a church.
2. Girls keep their heads covered in church.
They bow their heads when they pass a church.
3. They never chew gum or eat in church.
4. They try to be still when they sit.
5. They leave spaces between them
and the people who are next to them.
6. They never play in church.
7. Their feet are side by side when they stand.
8. They put money in the collection.
This helps to keep God's palace beautiful.
And sometimes it helps the poor.
9. They pray that the whole world will know
and love its great King.

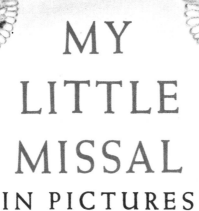

MY
LITTLE
MISSAL
IN PICTURES

by Reverend Francis Turmezei

Pictures by
Janet Robson Kennedy

IMPRIMATUR:
✠ JOHN GREGORY MURRAY, S.T.D.
ARCHBISHOP OF ST. PAUL
OCTOBER, 1950

The Church is God's House. God's Son, Jesus, is always on the altar. Jesus is waiting for you. He knows you and loves you. You can talk to Jesus just like . . .

. . . the little children talked to Him long ago when He lived on earth. Jesus is always glad to see you. And He blesses you.

When you are quiet and watch the priest at the altar, you are praying. You make God very happy by praying like this.

In the Mass we offer a gift to God with Jesus.
The angels come down from heaven
to pray with us.

At the beginning of Mass, the priest tells God that we are sorry for our sins. He does this when he bows down like the boy that Jesus told us about.

This boy ran away from home and became very naughty. Then one day he was sorry. He went home and asked his father to forgive him. The father did.

The priest raises his arms and says, "Glory be to God up in heaven!" Jesus is coming down to us again. That is why we are happy.

When Jesus came the first time the angels sang, "Glory be to God!" to the shepherds. That was the first Christmas.

The priest holds out his hands and begs God to give us what we need. God likes to help us. God wants us to ask Him for necessary things like . . .

. . . this mother who begged Jesus to make her little
girl well again. Because Jesus is God, He cured the
little girl.

Now the priest offers our gift to God. This is bread and wine. God is pleased when we offer our gift with a good heart.

Cain and Abel offered gifts to God. Abel had a kind
and loving heart and God was pleased with his gift.
Cain's heart was wicked and God did not like his gift.

God is pleased with our gift because Jesus offers it with us. So we are happy. And the priest expresses our joy by saying a prayer praising God.

In heaven the angels praise God before the throne of Jesus by singing the song, "Holy, holy, God is all holy."

The priest now prays for everybody in God's
family. This family is the Church. The Church is

the Pope, bishops, priests, and all the people who are joined with Jesus and do what He wants.

Now the priest is doing the same thing that Jesus did at the Last Supper. He is changing our gift into the Body and Blood of Jesus. Then he holds Jesus up so we can look at Him and say: "My Lord and my God."

At the Last Supper Jesus took bread and blessed
it and said: "This is My Body." Then He took wine
and blessed it saying: "This is My Blood." The bread
became His Body, the wine became His Blood.

The Body and Blood of Jesus is the very best Gift that we offer to God with the priest. Jesus also offers Himself to His Father again as . . .

. . . He did when He died on the Cross to open the gates of heaven again for all men. When Jesus gave His life, He made up for the sins of all men.

The priest now prays for all those in the great family of God who have died. He asks our Heavenly Father to give eternal happiness to the souls of the dead. After death we bury the body,

but the soul never dies. Many people go to purgatory when they die because they have not made up for their sins. We ask God to send the souls in purgatory to heaven.

Now the priest says the most holy of prayers—the *Our Father*—because . . .

. . . it is the one prayer that Jesus taught to His Apostles. That is why we say it so many times.

Jesus gave His Body and Blood to the Apostles at
the Last Supper. Now the priest gives Jesus to the
people to help them become better Christians
and to be happy with God in heaven one day.

This child has just received Jesus. His guardian angel is adoring Jesus Who is present in his heart. Ask Jesus to come into your heart by His love: "Come, my Jesus, I love you very much."

Through this blessing Jesus remains with us. He
goes out with us. He stays with us in our homes.

Here, the priest is blessing the people before they leave the Church.

When leaving the Church you should say: "That was beautiful, Jesus! I will be back soon."